What's for supper?

Qu'est-ce qu'on mange ce soir?

Mary Risk

Pictures by Carol Thompson
French by Christophe Dillinger

b small PUBLISHING

BILINGUAL BOOKS

We're cooking the supper tonight, Mum.

C'est *nous* qui allons préparer le dîner ce soir, maman.

It's going to be a surprise.

Ça va être une surprise.

Do we need cheese?

Il nous faut du fromage?

Yes, we need cheese, and ham too.

Oui, il nous faut du fromage et
aussi du jambon.

Do we need flour?

Il nous faut de la farine?

Yes.

Oui.

What about potatoes?
Do we need them?

Et des pommes de terre?
Il nous en faut?

No, we don't need potatoes.

Non, on n'a pas besoin de pommes de terre.

But we need tomatoes
and mushrooms.

Mais il nous faut des tomates et
des champignons.

Let's put some olives in it!

Mettons-y des olives!

Oh no! I don't like olives.

Ah non! Je n'aime pas les olives.

How much is all that?

C'est combien tout ça?

What are you going to make?
Please tell me. Please!

No! It's a surprise!

Qu'est-ce que vous allez préparer?
Allez, dites-moi, s'il vous plaît!

Non! C'est une surprise!

Here we are home again.

Nous voilà rentrés à la maison.

Don't come into the kitchen, Mum.

N'entre pas dans la cuisine, maman.

Supper's ready. It's…

Le dîner est prêt. C'est…

a pizza!

une pizza!

Pronouncing French

Don't worry if your pronunciation isn't quite correct. The important thing is to be willing to try. The pronunciation guide here will help but it cannot be completely accurate:

- Read the guide as naturally as possible, as if it were British English.

- Put stress on the letters in *italics*, e.g. from*aj*.

- Don't roll the r at the end of the word, for example in the French word **le** (the): ler.

If you can, ask a French person to help and move on as soon as possible to speaking the words without the guide.

Note French adjectives usually have two forms, one for masculine and one for feminine nouns. They often look very similar but are pronounced slightly differently, e.g. **prêt** and **prête** (see below).

Words Les Mots
leh moh

to cook supper
préparer le dîner
prehpah-*reh* ler deen*eh*

tonight
ce soir

ser swah

surprise
la surprise

lah s-yoor*preez*

cheese
le fromage

ler from*aj*

ham
le jambon

ler shom*boh*

flour
la farine

lah far-*een*

tomato
la tomate

lah tom*at*

potato
la pomme de terre

lah pom der *tair*

olive
l'olive

lol*eev*

mushroom
le champignon

ler shom-peen-*yoh*

pizza
la pizza

lah peet*zah*

ready
prêt/prête

preh/pret

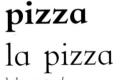

home/house
la maison
lah may*zoh*

mum
maman
ma-*moh*

dad
papa
pa-*pah*

kitchen
la cuisine
la kwee*zeen*

yes
oui
wee

no
non
noh

please
**s'il te plaît/
s'il vous plaî**
seel ter pleh/seel voo pleh

A simple guide to pronouncing this French story

Qu'est-ce qu'on mange ce soir?
*kesk*oh monsh ser swah

C'est *nous* qui allons préparer
seh *noo* kee al-*oh* prehpah-*reh*

le dîner ce soir, maman.
ler deen*eh* ser swah, ma-*moh*

Ça va être une surprise.
sah vah *etr'* yoon s-yoor*preez*

Il nous faut du fromage?
eel noo fo dew from*aj*

Oui, il nous faut du fromage
wee, eel noo fo dew from*aj*

et aussi du jambon.
eh oh*see* dew shom*boh*

Il nous faut de la farine?
eel noo fo der lah far-*een*

Oui.
wee

Et des pommes de terre?
et deh pom der *tair*

Il nous en faut?
eel noozoh fo

Non, on n'a pas besoin de pommes de terre.
noh, oh nah pah b'zwah der pom der *tair*

Mais il nous faut des tomates
meh eel noo fo deh tom*at*

et des champignons.
eh deh shom-peen-*yoh*

Mettons-y des olives!
met-o*zee* dezol*eev*

Ah non! Je n'aime pas les olives.
ah noh, sh' nem pah lezol*eev*

C'est combien tout ça?
seh kombee-*yah* too sah

Qu'est-ce que vous allez préparer?
kesker voozal-*eh* prehpah-*reh*

Allez, dites-moi, s'il vous plaît!
al-*eh*, deet mwah seel voo pleh

Non! C'est une surprise!
noh, set yoon s-yoor*preez*

Nous voilà rentrés à la maison.
noo vwah-*lah* ront*reh* ah lah may*zoh*

N'entre pas dans la cuisine, maman.
nontr' pah doh lah kwee*zeen*, ma-*moh*

Le dîner est prêt. C'est...
ler deen*eh* eh preh, seh

une pizza!
yoon peet*sah*

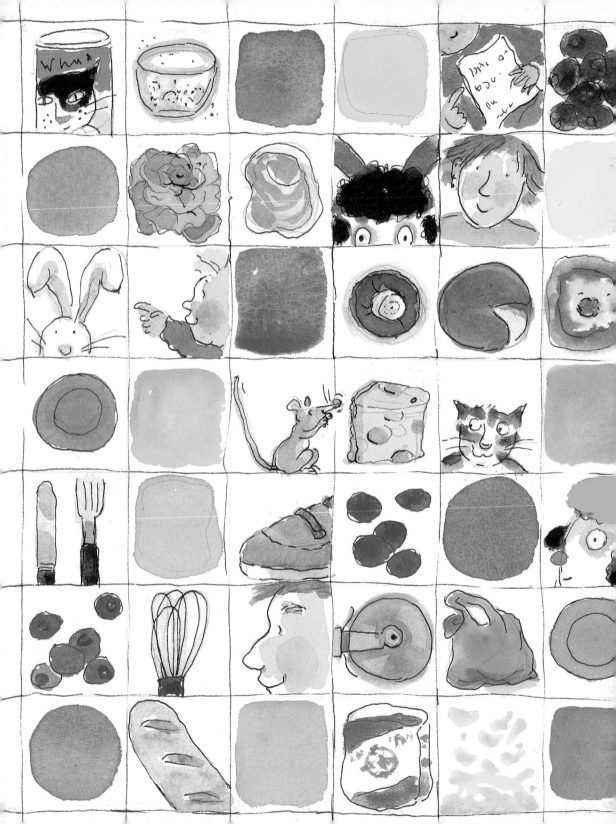